THE DREAMS BOOK

Distributed by Publishers Group West

THE DREAMS BOOK

FINDING OUR WAY THROUGH THE DARK

Technology for the Soul™

YEHUDA BERG

For further information:

The Kabbalah Centre
155 E. 48th St., New York, NY 10017
1062 S. Robertson Blvd., Los Angeles, CA 90035

1.800.Kabbalah www.kabbalah.com

First Edition
September 2004
Printed in USA
ISBN 1-57189-249-4

Design: Hyun Min Lee

DEDICATION

I dedicate this book to all the Kabbalists over the generations who, like my father and his teacher before him, suffered so, in order that all the people of the world would be able to use this technology to remove chaos from life.

TABLE OF CONTENTS

ACKNOWLEDGMENTS

I would like to thank the many people who have made this book possible.

First and foremost, Rav and Karen Berg, my parents and teachers. I will be forever thankful for your continual guidance, wisdom, and unconditional support. I am just one of the many whom you have touched with your love and wisdom.

Michael Berg, my brother, for your constant support and friendship, and for your vision and strength. Your presence in my life inspires me to become the best that I can be.

My wife, Michal, for your love and commitment; for your silent power; for your beauty, clarity, and uncomplicated ways. You are the strong foundation that gives me the security to soar.

David, Moshe, Channa, and Yakov, the precious gifts in

my life who remind me every day how much there is to be done to ensure that tomorrow will be better than today.

Billy Phillips, one of my closest friends, for your help in making this book possible. The contribution you make to the Kabbalah Centre every day and in so many ways is appreciated far more than you could possibly know.

To Andy Behrman, thank you for your consistent and passionate pursuit of truth and for committing your talents to helping our team make a difference in this world.

To Don Opper, Hyun Lee, Christian Witkin, and Esther Sibilia, whose contributions made the physical quality and integrity of everything we do live up to the spiritual heritage of this incredible wisdom that has been passed on to me by my father, Rav Berg.

To Lisa Mirchin, Courtney Taylor, Sharon Oberfeld, and Igor Iskiev—thank you for sharing your gifts in order that more people can access tools to discover their destiny.

I want to thank Rich Freese, Eric Kettunen, and all the team at PGW for their vision and support. Your proactive efficiency gives us the confidence to produce more and more books on Kabbalah so that the world can benefit from this amazing wisdom.

To all the Chevre at the Kabbalah Centres worldwide—the evenings we share together in study fuel my passion to bring the power of Kabbalah to the world. You are a part of me and my family no matter where you might be.

To the students who study Kabbalah all over the world—your desire to learn, to improve your lives, and to share with the world is an inspiration. The miracles I hear from you every day make everything I do worthwhile.

. . . I say to you today, my friends, that in spite of the difficulties and frustrations of the moment, I still have a dream. It is a dream deeply rooted in the American dream.

I have a dream that one day this nation will rise up and live out the true meaning of its creed: "We hold these truths to be self-evident: that all men are created equal." I have a dream that one day on the red hills of Georgia the sons of former slaves and the sons of former slaveowners will be able to sit down together at a table of brotherhood. I have a dream that one day even the state of Mississippi, a desert state, sweltering with the heat of injustice and oppression, will be transformed into an oasis of freedom and justice. I have a dream that my four children will one day live in a nation where they will not be judged by the color of their skin but by the content of their character. I have a dream today.

I have a dream that one day the state of Alabama, whose governor's lips are presently dripping with the words of interposition and nullification, will be transformed into a situation where little black boys and black girls will be able to join hands with little white boys and white girls and walk together as sisters and brothers. I have a dream today. I have a dream that one day every valley shall be exalted, every hill and mountain shall be made low, the rough places will be made plain, and the crooked places will be made straight, and the glory of the Lord shall be revealed, and all flesh shall see it together. This is our hope. This is the faith with which I return to the South. With this faith we will be able to hew out of the mountain of despair a stone of hope. With this faith we will be able to transform the jangling discords of our nation into a beautiful symphony of brotherhood. With this faith we will be able to work together, to pray together, to struggle together, to go to jail together, to stand up for freedom together, knowing that we will be free one day . . .

"I Have A Dream"
by Martin Luther King, Jr.

Delivered on the steps at the Lincoln Memorial in Washington D.C. on August 28, 1963. Source: *Martin Luther King, Jr: The Peaceful Warrior*, Pocket Books, NY 1968

DARE TO DREAM

Rav Berg, my father, had a very simple vision: He wanted to bring the teachings of Kabbalah to the people of the world without regard to their age, gender, or religion. For the religious establishment, however, this simple dream was considered unthinkable. For 20 centuries, the members of this establishment had jealously guarded Kabbalah's teachings and had used any means at their disposal—including violence—to keep them out of the hands of people like you and me.

So how was it possible for my father to realize his vision when 2000 years of deeply rooted protectiveness stood in his way?

It was possible because Destiny is stronger than Fear!

Thirty years ago, when my father first decided to manifest his dream, the teachings of Kabbalah were virtually unknown to anyone outside of a small number of Orthodox scholars. Even 15 years ago, despite my father's efforts, those teachings remained obscured behind a thick veil of secrecy, mystery, and mystification.

But then things began to change. As regular people began to drink from this infinite well of wisdom, my father's dream appeared in their hearts. They too wanted to share Kabbalah's wisdom with the world. Students became teachers. Teachers married and raised families. New Kabbalah learning centers sprang up all over the world, teaching the wisdom to adults and children. Lives were being transformed.

It was not without cost. Religious fanatics assaulted my mother, putting her in the hospital with a concussion. My brother and I were refused entry to school. My father was the object of a 30-year campaign of character assassination and threats. And all because he dared to envision a well of Kabbalistic knowledge that was open to everyone.

Today, Kabbalah has entered into the collective consciousness of the mainstream world. Kabbalah's teachings have been put to practical use by students from all walks of life. Scientists and physicians from around the world have used the teachings to remodel thinking about the universe and the human body. Miracles are becoming possible.

I share all this with you for one reason: to illustrate the power of a single dream. Persistence and never-ending belief in the dream are the keys to its manifestation in the world. And truthfully, the dream to bring Kabbalah to the world did not begin with my father. Nor did it begin with his teacher, Rav Yehuda Brandwein. Nor with Rav Brandwein's teacher, Rav Yehuda Ashlag. The dream has been passed down through a distinguished lineage of Kabbalists dating back some 2000 years to the greatest Kabbalist of them all: Rav Shimon bar Yochai. Rav bar Yochai gave the world the authentic Holy Grail—the *Zohar*, the most important book of Kabbalah. In this renowned book lay the secrets of Creation, the Big Bang origins of the universe, the knowledge of medicine and healing, the mysteries of our dreams, the secrets of our soul, and the techniques for achieving eternal happiness and fulfillment in a world overflowing with peace and prosperity.

Now I pass this dream on to you. I pass it on with the hope that you too will find your destiny in the nightly divine messages that we call Dreams.

—Yehuda Berg

INTRODUCTION

At one of our classes at the Kabbalah Centre in Los Angeles, a student related the following story:

> "Several years ago, I had a recurring dream. It always started with a big boom, like a loud gunshot. And then a voice telling me, '*You're not dead. You need to wake up. You need to drive the car.*' What car? There was no car in the dream! Nevertheless, because the voice sounded so urgent, I would try to wake up anyway. But no matter how hard I struggled in the dream, I couldn't do it. You understand, I would wake up *from* the dream but never *in* the dream. I had this dream several times over a period of about two weeks and was never able to wake up in the dream. And then finally I was able to do it—I woke myself up in the dream. And after that, I stopped having the dream.

"I had forgotten all about it, but one evening, a couple of weeks later, I was a passenger in a car driven by a friend, and I heard that boom, that loud gunshot, but I was unconscious. I didn't know why, but I was unconscious and I just wanted to sleep. Then I remembered that voice from the dream telling me, 'You're not dead. *You need to wake up. You need to drive the car.*' So I did—I woke myself up. I woke up to find that the car we were riding in was on fire; it had exploded, but we were still moving. I found out later that a huge tire had come off a semi-truck on the other side of the highway and had smashed into our car. Both my friend and I had immediately been knocked out, but my friend's foot was still pressing the accelerator. We were headed toward a head-on collision with oncoming traffic. But now I was awake. And as the voice had said, I needed '*to drive the car.*' And that's just what I did. Calmly, almost as though I was dreaming, I reached over from the passenger side and drove the car until we were safely out of the flow of traffic. I pulled over and parked.

"If I hadn't had that dream, I'm certain both my friend and I would be dead…"

This is the sort of story that mystifies, enthralls, and fascinates us. We all dream. And even though not all of us are fortunate enough to have had such a prophetic vision, we have all awakened in the middle of the night, consumed by images of an alternate reality in which the normal laws of time and space are suspended. All of us have awakened either terrified by a nightmare or inspired by images that bathe us in an overwhelming sense of peace and grace. In our dreams, we bear witness to bizarre events in eccentric places—some vaguely familiar, others so fantastic as to be the product of science fiction.

Since antiquity, dreams have given rise to numerous theories, conjectures, beliefs, and fears, both imaginative and scientific. They have been seen as a healing force, an extension of the waking state, and a source of divination.

So what are dreams? Where do they come from? Can dreams be reduced to mere unconscious representations of our personal hopes and fears? Are they no more than the peculiar effect on our delicate metabolism of one too many late-night Fatburgers? Are they only a replay of random images and noise?

Or do dreams come to us from a higher place? In other words . . .

. . . are our dreams trying to tell us something?

The answers to these questions—and many more—can be found in an ancient body of wisdom that dates back to the beginning of time.

That ancient body of wisdom is called Kabbalah.

TECHNOLOGY OF THE SOUL OR THE THEORY OF EVERYTHING

Kabbalah is the oldest and most influential body of knowledge in the world. It is a discipline that reveals both the spiritual and physical laws that govern the universe and the human soul. More significantly, Kabbalah is an *applied* science—a body of knowledge with practical application in the real world. It gives answers to our most fundamental questions: Why are we here, where did we come from, how should we conduct ourselves, what is our purpose in life?

The Theory of Everything

Albert Einstein coined the term *unified field theory* shortly after developing the theory of relativity. Put succinctly, unified field theory is the long-sought means of tying together all known phenomena to explain the nature and behavior of all matter and energy in existence. As a result, it is often called the *Theory of Everything*. Physicists have surmised that such a concept, if proven, would unlock all the secrets of nature and make myriad wonders possible, including such practical benefits as time travel and an inexhaustible source of clean energy. According to Michio Kaku, a theoretical physicist at City College, City University of New York, those in pursuit of the Theory of Everything seek "an equation an inch long that would allow us to read the mind of God."

Kabbalah is the Theory of Everything. Its application provides solutions to difficult questions that go unanswered by other, less inclusive disciplines. It unravels life's puzzles. It deciphers codes. And, like all sciences, Kabbalah uncovers the miraculous order and harmony in what often appears to be the chaos of life. It gives practical tools to effect authentic change in our lives and in the world. It tells us that things happen *for a reason*.

A Little History

The pedigree of Kabbalah stretches far back in the historical record. Abraham the Patriarch wrote its first text, *The Book of Formation*, some 4000 years ago. Effectively, *The Book of Formation* is that "inch-long" equation to which Michio Kaku referred. Although only a few pages in length, *The Book of Formation* contains the answers to all the mysteries of the Universe. Like the equation $E = MC^2$, these ancient pages reveal a vast amount of information in a highly condensed form. And like Einstein's famous equation, very few people are able to fully understand its profound implications.

Like life-giving water locked away in the form of ice at the top of a remote mountain, the wisdom contained in *The Book of Formation* remained inaccessible for almost 2000 years. Then, in the 2nd century, in Israel, Rabbi Shimon bar Yochai took it upon himself to decode its knowledge. The result was a multivolume manuscript in verse form called *The Book of Splendor*, or the *Zohar*. The *Zohar* is a work of unequaled wisdom and spiritual power. It expresses ideas encoded in *The Book of Formation* that were centuries ahead of their time. In an age when everyone believed that the Earth was flat, the *Zohar* described our planet as spherical. It depicted the moment of creation as a Big Bang–like explosion. It explored the notion of parallel universes. It effectively predicted the most current scientific model of a physical universe of 10 dimensions. But as science writer Arthur C. Clarke has said, "Any sufficiently advanced technology is indistinguishable from magic." In the 2nd century, the *Zohar* was considered a heretical text. Clearly, the world was not ready for it; the thaw had not yet begun. So the wisdom and knowledge it contained remained frozen on that mountaintop.

In the 13th century, in Spain, Rav Moses de Leon rediscovered the *Zohar*. His discovery, however, went largely unnoticed by the general public as well as by most of the more advanced minds of his generation. Still, Rav discover marked a change in climate. The ice was warming.

In the 16th century, Rav Isaac Luria produced a historic commentary on the *Zohar* that rescued this unique body of wisdom from obscurity. Luria's commentary and teachings became the definitive school of Kabbalistic thought. Scholars soon translated Luria's writings into Latin, which allowed the wisdom of the

Zohar to influence some of the greatest thinkers of the Renaissance—including Isaac Newton and Gottfried Leibniz. The *Zohar's* wisdom, frozen for so many years, began to flow down to the world.

All the insights in this book are rooted in the Lurianic commentaries.

HIDE AND SEEK

"It's a fairly embarrassing situation to admit that we can't find 99 percent of the universe."

> —Bruce Margon, PhD, Associate Director for
> Science, Space Telescope Science Institute,
> Baltimore, Maryland

One of the most important and innovative insights offered by the *Zohar* is its conception that "reality"—what we can see, touch, taste, smell, and feel—represents only 1 percent of the complete picture of the universe. In this regard, the *Zohar* joins with modern astronomers like Dr. Bruce Margon, who now estimate that nearly 99 percent of the physical universe is hidden from view. "Mother Nature is having a double laugh," Dr. Margon tells us. "She's hidden most of the matter in the universe, and hidden it in a form that can't be seen."

To the Kabbalist, this little joke is fundamental to

understanding how the world really works. It is an essential principle when considering the nature of our task, our job, and our mission in life.

A World of Shadow—A Realm of Light
1 Percent/99 Percent

So what is this 1 percent of the universe that we call "reality"?

Put simply, it is the world we see every day. It is what we perceive with our five senses. It is the physical world. It is the familiar world of subways, job interviews, and romance. It is a world of Type A behavior, B-ball, and the G spot—a world of wonder and accidents, longing and unforeseen turmoil. It is the "vale of tears" to which so many poets have referred. It is, as Shakespeare wrote, that "brief candle" with birth at one end and death at the other.

But just as modern science tells us that there is far more matter and energy in the universe than we can see, so too does the *Zohar* tell us that there is much more to life than this 1 percent world in which we are so completely enmeshed. In fact, this 1 percent reality is only a shadow—*a three-dimensional shadow*—of a 10-dimensional reality that is hidden from our immediate senses!

Let's say that again:

The 1 percent world is merely a shadow of a higher reality.

Like all shadows, the 1 percent world doesn't even exist without the 99 percent world. In fact, nothing happens in our 1 percent world that does not begin in the 99 percent world. The 99 percent world is the source, the fountainhead, the first cause of all that happens. All knowledge, wisdom, and joy dwell within its realm. It is here that true fulfillment, enduring peace, and lasting satisfaction reside. It is the realm of Light.

But let's admit it—like the astronomers looking for the vast amount of physical matter that is hidden from our view, most of us find ourselves in the embarrassing position of having to admit that we can't find this well-spring of enduring peace, fulfillment, and satisfaction. Oh sure, we do get fleeting glimpses of it. We find love, financial success, or a new job, and we briefly feel satisfied. But then, in a flash, it's gone. This is because in the 1 percent world, we get only *momentary* satisfaction, *fleeting* happiness, and *temporary* gratification. So we continue striving, struggling, fighting to recreate that feeling. But it seems as if we can never make it last. And that's because . . .

. . . we are trying to manipulate a shadow. We are literally focusing our attention in the wrong place. *Lasting* peace, *lasting* fulfillment, *lasting* satisfaction can't be found in the shadow realm of the 1 percent world. In fact, the pleasures and contentment that we find in the 1 percent world are only a hint—a mere inkling of the much more substantial happiness and fulfillment that are to be found in the Light of the 99 percent world.

But here's that little joke again.

The 99 percent world is hidden.

And it is hidden from us *by design.*

By design? Yes. Deliberately? Yes.

The 99 percent world is hidden from us for a reason.

It is hidden from us *in order that we may, by our own choice and through our own efforts, seek it out.*

The Old-Fashioned Way

Several years ago there was a popular television commercial for an investment bank that claimed, "We make money the old-fashioned way—we *earn* it." Kabbalah teaches that spiritual riches must likewise be earned. The design of the universe dictates and requires that we engage in a daily struggle against our natural egocentric tendency to pursue only those things that enrich us. By our own choice and through our own efforts, we must overcome what comes most naturally to us. To be sure, this is not an easy thing to do—but that is exactly the point. Kabbalah teaches that what comes easily to us has little value. Unearned wealth—be it spiritual or material—is more likely to bring regret or embarrassment than lasting joy or fulfillment.

Put simply, the only thing that stands in the way of accessing the 99 percent world is ourselves. By struggling against our 1 percent nature, we begin the process of entering the Light of the hidden 99 percent. This is what it's all about. And don't bother complaining about the idea of *earning before reaping your destined rewards*. According to Kabbalah, it was you and I who asked for the opportunity to genuinely earn all the joy and happiness that is our ultimate destiny. The souls of humanity desired an arrangement in which effort and striving would first be required before one could actually hold up the championship trophy. When you stop and think about it, it makes sense. After all, would anyone really want to win a championship trophy without ever having played a single game? "Playing the game"—striving to win over a long and grueling season while overcoming real obstacles—is what gives meaning and purpose to the concepts of winning and victory. So our 1 percent nature is our actual opponent, and accessing that 99 percent at will is the ultimate objective of the game. Thankfully, however, we have a few tools to help us reach that goal.

Accessing the Hidden World

The *Zohar* is the guidebook, the operating manual, the toolkit we use to access the hidden world. It supplies the techniques for seeing past the shadows of the 1 percent and revealing the Light of the 99 percent. It gives us the means of discovering that concealed fountainhead out of which all joys and successes flow. It explains how we may "log in" to the 99 percent world and, more significantly, how we can stay connected to that world in order to lead a fulfilling and involved life.

The *Zohar* provides us with hundreds of ways to connect to this hidden world.

And one of the most powerful ways happens when we are asleep.

SOUL FOOD

When a man sleeps in his bed, his soul leaves him to soar above, each soul according to its own way . . .
　—The *Zohar*

As the world becomes more and more dependent on portable computers, cell phones, and PDAs, it becomes almost second nature for us, every night, to plug in these electronic devices so that they will have the power to assist us during the day. Without a recharge, our electronic collaborators would be useless.

In much the same way, the soul must connect to its source each night in order to collaborate with us as we wend our way through life. When we sleep, the *Zohar* tells us, a major portion of our soul leaves our body in the 1 percent world to "plug in" to the 99 percent realm. Just enough of the soul is left behind to keep our bodies safe from harm.

Sleep, then, is not merely a time for the body to rest; it

is a time for the soul to access the source of its power. Without this recharge, without sleep, we become lethargic and confused. We are unable to concentrate. We become depressed. The "light" seems to have gone out of our lives. And, in fact, without sleep, this is exactly what happens—our soul becomes cut off from the Light and is unable to revitalize and renew itself, unable to send strong signals to lead us along our unique spiritual path. The soul is our spiritual positioning device, but if it should be cut off from its source of power, its positive influence on our daily life weakens.

From this we begin to understand that our soul is actually a part of the hidden world, a small fragment of the greater Light. This fragment resides within each of us. As such, while we have life, the soul can never be completely extinguished. The soul—this fragment of the Light— is our inheritance, our birthright, our hope, and our potential. And we, in turn, are its custodians. We can nourish and nurture this potential, and it will grow. Or we can ignore it and, through neglect, watch its influence dwindle to a faint whisper of its potential power.

Finding Our Way

The *Zohar* teaches us that we have all come into this world in order to nourish and nurture our connection to the hidden 99 percent world. To do this, we must all go through a process of constant change and improvement. Since we live in the 1 percent world, it is only through our own actions here that we can demonstrate these changes.

But how do we know which way to go? How do we uncover the correct path? In a world cluttered with deadlines and mortgages, gas bills and groceries, how do we see our way clear to the urgings of our conscience, our soul?

Wouldn't it be nice if we could get periodic communications from the 99 percent world that reassured us when we were moving in the right direction or warned us when our bearings had faltered?

The *Zohar* tells us that we do, in fact, receive these communications.

They are called Dreams.

"You've Got Mail"

Every dream is a message from the 99 percent world. During our waking hours, a constant struggle is waged between the physical consciousness of the body, which seeks the material satisfaction of the 1 percent world, and the consciousness of the soul, which aspires to the higher 99 percent realm. But during sleep, this dynamic changes. During sleep, body consciousness is released, and the soul is set free to revisit a realm that lies beyond time and space. Dreams are messages that we receive when we are least attached to the 1 percent world—when our souls are elevated. A dream is our own private navigational instrument, helping us plot a course through the storms of daily life. And because of this, every dream deserves our attention.

It is important to recognize, however, that some dreams are more attached to the 99 percent world than others. The *Zohar* tells us that there are several levels of dreams. Like e-mail, a dream may have a low priority, a normal priority, or a high priority. Some dreams might even be categorized as "junk mail." And, depending on the spiritual nature of the dreamer, each dream has at least a little mixture of designations. Even the highest-priority dream may have some junk attached.

"1 Percent," or "Natural," Dreams

The lowest form of dream is what we call the "1 percent," or "Natural," dream. This is a dream that is mostly attached to the 1 percent world of our daily experience. When we are running a fever and dream of fires, this is certainly a 1 percent dream. When we are overstressed at work and dream of being pursued by an unseen enemy, there is a good chance that this is a 1 percent dream. Daydreams commonly fit into this category as well. Natural dreams are directly related to the stresses, anxieties, and pressures that we experience during our waking life. They are more like psychic echoes of experience than genuine peeks into the future or hints about our destiny. Natural dreams are quite frequent and widespread, and they serve the useful purpose of releasing tension and allowing us an additional perspective on which to lean. But they are a sign that the soul has not completely elevated during sleep; the physical world, the 1 percent world, still dominates the message.

"99 Percent," or "Providence," Dreams

Dreams on the middle level are called "99 percent," or "Providence," dreams. They occur when the soul has made a good connection to the 99 percent world and we receive messages that contain important lessons or warnings about our spiritual health, our destiny, and the future. A Providence dream offers us an opportunity to discover what we need to change and correct in order to elevate ourselves in our daily lives.

A Providence dream comes from a realm in which our past, present, and future are all interwoven into one fabric. In the 99 percent realm, the future has already occurred. As a result, the message we receive in a Providence dream gives us a glimpse of what lies ahead—or, more to the point, lends insight into the eventual consequences of our present actions.

Imagine that you are hiking through a thick forest and

you have a "spotter" flying overhead in a helicopter. This spotter can tell you where your path is taking you, if there are any obstacles ahead, or whether your route ends in a deadly morass. Surely it would be folly to ignore the advice of the spotter. In much the same way, the *Zohar* tells us that it is reckless to ignore the guidance of a Providence dream.

The relevant symbols of a Providence dream are often intermingled with the insignificant and the confusing. Nevertheless, every effort should be made to remember a Providence dream. Fortunately, it is not uncommon for us to awaken in the middle of the night after having such a dream. You should write Providence dreams down in as much detail as possible even when their images make little immediate sense to you. A qualified teacher or interpreter will be able to sort out the wheat from the chaff. It is in the details that the meaning of these dreams will be found.

"Prophetic" Dreams

The highest dreams are called "Prophetic" dreams. These dreams are usually very clear and unambiguous and are easily remembered. As their name implies, Prophetic dreams are those that accurately foresee the future. They are the result of a complete connection to the 99 percent realm and are usually received by those who have made a lifelong commitment to spiritual transformation.

The *Zohar* tells us that our souls rise and connect to the 99 percent realm "according to our merit." None of us is born perfect. Each of us has unique obstacles to overcome. We are here on this Earth to perfect ourselves. Individuals who devote their waking hours to revealing the 99 percent realm through selfless acts of sharing and charity—who work hard to change and improve—will see their souls reach heights that are unattainable to those who are less committed. Positive actions arouse prophetic messages of truth, while negative behaviors invoke deceitful messages and disingenuous dreams. Put another way, we reap what we sow. A Prophetic dream comes only to those who have earned it.

There are two kinds of Prophetic dreams—Positive and Negative. A Positive Prophetic dream foretells of some good that will occur. A Negative Prophetic dream threatens chaos, destruction, or disease. Positive prophecy is immutable; it *will* happen. Negative prophecy can, on the other hand, be acted upon and changed.

Nightmares

Generally, a nightmare is an urgent message signaling that a change of direction is needed. A nightmare is like a big yellow caution sign on life's highway, telling us to slow down, pull over, and think about what we're doing in the world.

Negative behavior in the world has consequences. Greed, self-indulgence, vindictiveness, and anger have consequences. It is important to understand, however, that a nightmare is NOT a consequence. It is merely a caution, a warning, that danger lies ahead. As frightening as a nightmare may be, it is only a sign. The real consequences of our negativity are much worse than mere nightmares. Diseases, anxiety, financial distress, even bad luck are all consequences of our own negative actions or lack of positive actions in the world. The *Zohar* tells us that we are ultimately responsible for almost everything that happens to us.

Or, to put it another way, "What goes around comes around."

A nightmare, then, is actually a blessing. Like a well-placed Caution sign, a nightmare is often the only thing that prevents us from crashing into a brick wall or running off the road. If we heed the warning it gives us—if we take vigorous measures to stop our negative actions—we will avoid the real pain, insecurity, and fear in our daily lives that the nightmare has only implied.

The Soul Channel

Modern scientific sleep studies have determined that sleep consists of different stages, some of which bear a closer resemblance to wakefulness than others. The *Zohar*, too, has identified several stages of sleep but offers us a different perspective on the same facts.

The *Zohar* tells us that as night falls, the soul begins to elevate and is gradually released from the grip of the 1 percent world of our bodies—of ego and selfish desires—to reunite with the 99 percent world. Reflecting this dynamic, the quality and the quantity of messages that we receive from the upper world increase as the night progresses. As the soul rises, the connection gets better and better.

Think of it this way: Imagine that the 99 percent world had a TV station, the Soul Channel, and the 1 percent world had a TV station, the Illusion Channel. Both stations broadcast 24 hours a day, seven days a week. The Soul Channel broadcasts a full complement of *compelling* educational programming that is specifically targeted to each viewer. If the two of us are tuned into the Soul Channel, what you see is different from what I see.

The Illusion Channel, on the other hand, broadcasts the same thing to everyone—news, sitcoms, sports, drama, and a lot of advertising for products that promise to make us instantly thinner, richer, and more beautiful. It's entertaining, it's captivating, and, more than anything else, it's noisy. When we're tuned into the Illusion Channel, hardly anything else can get our attention.

At night, however, an opportunity opens up for each of us. With sleep, we seem to get better reception of the Soul Channel. It's not that the signal has gotten any stronger; to the contrary, it has remained the same. What has changed is *us*. With the loss of body consciousness, the noise and tumult of the Illusion Channel fade, and our "receiver"—our soul—advances to the higher frequency at which the Soul Channel broadcasts its signal. Our "receiver"—the soul—rises to meet that signal, which has been there all along.

The *Zohar* tells us that the hours between 2 A.M. and dawn are the best times to receive a clear picture from the Soul Channel. It is during these hours that we are least tuned in to our bodies and most tuned in to the soul. Additionally, Friday evenings and Saturday afternoons are particularly advantageous for connection. During these times, the broadcast signal is "amped up," creating a bonus opportunity to pick up the information we need to transform ourselves.

DREAM MANAGEMENT

The *Zohar* offers a host of techniques with which to improve the clarity and efficacy of our dreams. It should be clear by now, however, that the responsibility for progress in this, as in every spiritual aspiration, rests with us. To develop the quality of our dreams, to improve our lives both spiritually and materially, we need to *transform ourselves*.

How often do we hear people say, "*I want to be different. I want to feel lasting satisfaction and peace. I want less chaos in my life, less anxiety.*" These longings are reasonable, but what people usually mean is this: "*I want to be different. Just don't ask me to change.*"

The *Zohar* tells us that we all have the ability to change our behavior and the world. It is well within our power to do so. And by changing our behavior, we move closer to that fountainhead of lasting peace and satisfaction. By being honest with ourselves—by rooting out self-delusion, anger, bigotry, greed, resentment, willfulness, and self-importance—and, even more critically, by *helping others*—we take the necessary steps toward clearing the way to the Hidden World.

Make no mistake, however: This transformation objective is not in any way, shape, or form motivated by the concepts of morals or ethics. Not at all. To the contrary, it is based on the concept of *greed*. Greed? Yes, greed—but not for the illusionary, fleeting pleasures that gratify our ego. You can be sure that if greed for the ego delivered endless, eternal fulfillment, Kabbalists throughout history would have been the most egocentric, self-indulgent people on the planet. But gratification for the ego always includes chaos somewhere down the line. It comes at a cost. Thus, Kabbalists shift their greed from that of ego to that of the soul—from the temporary pleasures of the 1 percent to the eternal joys that flow from the 99 percent. So the next time you realize that you have to change a negative aspect of your nature, do not be motivated by morals and ethics. Recognize, instead, that it's a smart and shrewd investment that pays dividends into eternity.

And understand the Kabbalistic principle that says if we want to "plug in" to the 99 percent realm to experience authentic pleasure and fulfillment that does not wear off, we must first do the "grunt work."

Before Sleep

The *Zohar* tell us that when we awaken in the morning, we are reborn. We are literally a new creation. If this is so, however, how is it that we still carry so much "baggage" from the day before? Why do we continue to feel anxious, angry, or depressed almost as soon as we have opened our eyes?

The answer is that we have neglected to take out the "garbage" the night before. That "garbage" is our own negativity, our lack of kindness to others, our neglect of our spiritual mission. Disposing of this "garbage" requires that we turn our thoughts inward and take responsibility for our actions.

Before going to bed, before sleep, we should take a few moments to earnestly contemplate and question the way we behaved during the day. How could we have been more helpful to others? Where did we stumble over our own pride, selfishness, or impatience? Could we have been more loving or sympathetic to our partners or coworkers? Did we react with passion when we ought to have shown compassion? What amends can we make to rectify our errors? What actions can we take in the days ahead to bring us closer to the 99 percent world?

Introspective questions such as these point to a responsible and sincere desire to transform ourselves. By proactively evaluating our behavior each night and taking responsibility for our daily actions, we clear out the negative trash that prevents the soul from fully connecting to the 99 percent realm in which we can find the guidance that we seek. The more specific our questions, the more accurate the dream answers will be.

Yet another tool for establishing a clear soul connection can be found in Prayer and Meditation. We suggest a meditation that focuses on a special three-letter combination of Aramaic letters from the 72 Names of God. The Kabbalists explain that the 22 letters of the Aramaic alphabet are the "spiritual DNA" behind all matter. These 22 letters existed before Creation, and were used as mediums to transfer energy from the Upper Worlds – the 99% – to our physical 1% world. These three letters—Lamed, Lamed, and Hey—have a specific energy related to dreams.

Although even a simple scan of the letters above will have a cleansing effect, we suggest that you set aside time to concentrate on them while directing your attention to the following meditation:

You are at peace.

As you fall asleep, clear your mind and allow the Light to enter your dreams.

Let your soul open to truth, to love. Feel its ascension.

Let go of daily chaos, renewal is yours.

You awaken in the morning elevated and recharged. Body and spirit wiser.

During Sleep

Some of us may find that we are able to direct or change our dreams *as they are happening*. This is a gift that is usually reserved for those who have attained a very high level of spiritual transformation. Nevertheless, all of us can train for this ability by focusing our attention, as we are falling asleep, on a specific spiritual question or problem. As we drift off, the soul, carrying our questions, is released from the bond of the body and arrives at the exact location where answers and solutions are found. Truly evolved and enlightned individuals have the ability to put these answers to work *while they are dreaming*. Elevated people can transform negativity on the spot, thereby preventing it from entering the 1 percent world. The rest of us, however, must apply the solutions we find in dreams only when we reemerge into the waking world.

Afterwards

Be proactive. We see dreams for a reason. If you are fortunate enough to receive a clear message in your dreams, put the information to work. Simply knowing the answer isn't the end of the job. The hard part, for all of us, is making the changes suggested by the dream. But remember: The more difficult the change, the more Light will be revealed.

The most difficult changes are often those we must make internally—a commitment to resist anger, envy, or other negative emotions that have become second nature to us. Ridding ourselves of negative emotions requires us to short-circuit behaviors that supply us with a "real charge" but leave us feeling worn out and in shock. Resisting these behaviors opens a new channel to the Upper World, where the real power source is located.

Removing Judgment

Frightening dreams are unforgettable. Fortunately, the *Zohar* provides several techniques with which to transform the negativity suggested by such dreams.

The first method is remarkably simple: Help somebody else. This can take the form of a "good deed" such as volunteering at a hospital or a homeless shelter, or donating money or time to someone in need. The opportunities for charitable work are everywhere. They might also include simple unexpected acts of sharing with our friends or, better yet, our enemies. Regardless, it is best to do this in the morning following the dream, or as soon as possible thereafter.

In the event of an extremely negative dream, there are specific actions that can be taken to lessen the chances of its realization. For more information about these procedures, contact the nearest Kabbalah Centre.

INTERPRETING DREAMS

Opportunity Knocking

Dreams offer us a unique opportunity to change, adjust, and transform our consciousness. As we make these corrections, we strengthen our connection to the 99 percent world, making it possible to receive even clearer dreams and more fulfillment in our lives. In other words, the more "down and dirty" transformational work we do during the day, the more elevated the soul can be at night. Similarly, the more elevated the soul at night, the clearer will be the signs we receive about our daily adjustments. In short, dreams afford us the chance for an ever-rising spiral of spiritual transformation and an ever-increasing wattage of spiritual Light to enter our lives.

But in order to take advantage of this opportunity, we have to know what our dreams are telling us. If we do not understand the messages that are being conveyed through our dreams, we miss out on the specific path of correction that we came to this world to achieve. If negative situations remain unresolved and if our character remains unchanged, the door will be left wide open for chaos and negativity to manifest in our lives.

Clearly, the correct interpretation of a dream is extremely important.

In fact, the *Zohar* tells us that *the interpretation of the dream is more important than the dream itself.*

A Cautionary Tale

The sages of antiquity tell us that there were 24 dream interpreters in Jerusalem at the time of the Second Temple, around 2000 years ago. A man visited every one of the interpreters and told each of them the same dream. To his surprise, he received 24 different interpretations! But, even more astonishingly, *all of the interpretations came true!*

How can this be? If all the interpretations were different, how could all of them have been correct?

The answer is that all of them were NOT correct. The truth is that even a mistaken interpretation of a dream can be manifested in the world. Or, as the *Zohar* says:

"A dream contains truth and lies; hence, the words of interpretation prevail over everything, in that they determine whether the true or the false part shall prevail."

Think of it in this way: Every symbol in a dream has potential energy, and the interpretation activates that potential in the world. If we have a good dream and we do not tell it to an interpreter, that dream remains in a state of potential—that is to say, the positive energy of the dream will not manifest in the world, and an opportunity for transformation will have been lost. As distressing as this may seem, it is even more worrisome if a negative or incorrect interpretation is activated. Caution should thus be taken when we choose an interpreter, because an interpretation that is incorrect or negative can be activated in the world just as assuredly as can a positive or accurate one.

Choosing an Interpreter

Two factors should be considered when choosing a person to interpret your dreams:

1. Choose someone who loves you.

A person who truly loves us will always interpret a dream in its most positive light. Or, as the *Zohar* puts it:

"We have learned that when a man has had a dream, he should unburden himself of it before men who are his friends so that they should express to him their good wishes and give utterances to words of good omen."

"Thus, a man's friends should affirm the good interpretation, and so all will be well."

Keep in mind that this is not always as easy as it appears. Even our closest friends and loved ones may unconsciously attach a meaning to a dream that has more to do with *their* deepest hopes and fears than with ours. We're all guilty of this. It is very difficult to keep our egos at bay when we hear a friend's dream; it is difficult to take our selves out of the interpretation. A purely selfless interpretation requires a level of altruism and charity that not everyone has attained. Which brings us to the second factor to consider when choosing an interpreter . . .

2. Choose someone with a high level of spirituality.

The person we choose to interpret our dream should be knowledgeable about the spiritual realm and about the concepts of dream interpretation. Individuals who have committed themselves to spiritual change, who do the work that is required to elevate the soul and reveal the 99 percent world, are those who can offer an interpretation that is both positive and illuminating. Because of their knowledge and level of spirituality, they are able to activate the most positive energy possible even in the most negative dream.

Clearly, a person who combines the qualities of friendship and is elevated spiritually is the ideal choice. Often these traits can be found in a respected teacher—

someone who is familiar with us personally and spiritually, and who understands both our aspirations and our faults.

DREAM SYMBOLS AND THEIR INTERPRETATION

Kabbalistic dream interpreters advise against applying inflexible rules to the meaning of a particular symbol in a dream. The context of each symbol, as well as the dreamer's personality, history, and recent circumstances, can modify or even reverse its meaning. As the old proverb says, "One man's meat is another man's poison." In other words, the appearance of a snake in a dream may have different meanings for different people depending on the unique events of the dream and the character of the dreamer. This is further complicated by symbols seen in combination. For these reasons, we should never interpret a dream by ourselves. Instead, we should write the dream down in as much detail as possible and seek the help of a qualified teacher. And remember:

Negative dreams can be acted upon and changed.

A negative dream is not absolute; it is a call to action. No matter what the particulars of the message, we have the ability and the strength to turn the negative to a positive, to transform our conduct in the world, to overcome weakness. We are never asked to transform that wich we are not equipped to change.

The following examples are only a preliminary guide.

Plants

Trees
Trees are very powerful symbols. Uprooted or fallen trees are almost always a cautionary sign of impending trouble, panic, or conflict either for the dreamer or for the community. Climbing a tree is an indication of upcoming honor in your life. A tree in bloom is a positive sign indicating good fortune. When we see fruit on a tree, it is usually a call to con-

nect and collaborate with a noteworthy person who is symbolized by the tree.

Wheat and Barley

Dreams that contain wheat and barley are almost always positive. Wheat heralds improved circumstances and peace. Barley foretells reversed negativity and indicates a transformation of our behavior and correction of past mistakes.

Animals

The interpretation of animal symbols often depends on the dreamer's relationship to the animal in the dream. If, for example, you are leading the animal, the interpretation is different from what it would be if you were being pursued by it.

Lion

If we see ourselves winning a struggle with a

lion, it foretells our success over an adversary. If, on the other hand, we see ourselves lying down with a lion, it indicates that our enemy will become our friend and that peace will prevail between us.

Deer

Deer almost always symbolize innocence. Killing a deer in a dream is a warning to be wary of shedding innocent blood and can also indicate a danger of hurting someone, physically or emotionally, who does not deserve it. If we receive a deer as a gift, happiness and prominence are in store for us.

Birds

Almost all species of birds, with the possible exceptions of the owl and the pelican, are favorable signs. Geese portend honor and wisdom. Capturing a hawk in a dream is a sign of impending good fortune. The mere sighting of an eagle in flight foretells great prominence and respect. A raven flying toward us is an assurance of upcoming spiritual or physical sustenance.

Eggs

Eggs represent a dreamer's desire or aspiration. An unbroken egg generally indicates a desire that remains unfulfilled or a request or need that remains unresolved. A broken egg foretells a request granted, a hope realized. The same is true of anything that can be broken open, such as a walnut or a glass jar or vase. Whole, their contents remain hidden; broken, their contents are revealed.

Elements

Water

Water has many different meanings depending on the context. Sometimes it carries a meaning of purification; at other times it denotes inundation, loss of control, and chaos. A dream of a refreshing rain is generally a sign of improved circumstances or good news. If we see ourselves drinking clear, clean water, it is very positive, indicating tranquillity, joy, and peace, especially if the water is taken from a spring or a well. Swimming in a calm sea or swimming pool is also a positive sign, indicating an upcoming union with spiritually enlightened people. Rushing or roiled water, on the other hand, is considered negative, a harbinger of difficulties.

Earth

If we are in good health and see ourselves digging in or carrying soil, the dream is generally neutral. If we are in ill health, it is a cautionary sign about our physical condition, signifying that action is required on our part to correct an underlying physical or spiritual weakness.

Fire

Fire is considered a destructive and untamed force, and a dream of fire may indicate problems for the community, the nation, or the dreamer. If we see our own house a blaze, for example, this generally indicates an impending dispute or an argument. On the other hand, fire that is domesticated for our own use, such as a candle or a fireplace, denotes spirituality. Lighting a candle in a dream is a positive sign; snuffing one out is negative.

Wind

Wind, too, has a dual nature, depending on its context. Being swept up in a wind may herald a rise to a position in which we exercise authority or command over others. By contrast, a malevolent wind may warn of devastation, illness, or disputes.

A Sample Dream and Interpretation

A student at the Kabbalah Centre described the following dream:

> "I was in the living room of my house, wearing a green T-shirt and sandals. An evil-looking wild animal climbed down the wall of the room and walked toward me. The animal then transformed into a cat, and then into a lion that looked right through me. Frightened, I woke up. It was 3:30 in the morning."

An understanding of the personality and circumstances of the dreamer is a distinct advantage in dream interpretation. In this case, I had the good fortune of knowing the student well. He was a person who worked diligently to transform himself spiritually, had a successful business with his brother, was in good health, and had a sound and stable relationship with his wife and children.

I began by asking the student to remember as many

details of the dream as possible and learned that the images were very clear, with vibrant colors. The clarity of a dream is often a good indication of its level of truthfulness; the greater the clarity, the more truthful the dream. Because the images were clear and because I knew this student to be spiritually sincere and conscientious, I suspected that the dream was indeed a truthful warning of an upcoming problem. It was evident that the dream had frightened the student, but from his body language I sensed that his fear was not the deep "soul" fear that is commonly associated with an extremely negative prophecy. In other words, his dream was warning him of a problem that needed to be addressed, but neither he nor his family members were in grave danger.

I then asked the student if he had "directed" his dream in any way before going to sleep. Had he asked a particular question? He responded that he hadn't, but he did recall that he had been hoping, in a general way, for guidance about the company that he owned with his brother. This was a key piece of information that allowed me to begin peeling off the layers of the dream to reveal its core meaning.

The essential message of the dream was rooted in the transformation of the three animals—wild animal to cat to lion. Because this transition took place in the living room of the student's house—a room deeply associated with the family—I knew the dream was family focused. Since he had mentioned that he was seeking guidance about his business, and since I knew he was in business with his brother, I felt strongly that he had received a message that addressed this area of his life.

The first animal in the student's dream was a wild animal, a frightening beast. This is a common dream symbol that refers to an enemy or adversary who is conspiring against or lying to us. This animal turned into a cat. A cat can mean that a decree or a judgment is removed. Negativity enters our lives because of negative actions or spiritual inaction on our part. The wild animal turning into a cat indicated that the negativity of the conspiring adversary would be removed. This idea was amplified by the transformation of the cat into a peaceful lion, a symbol of a triumph over adversity.

Specifically, the dream was warning this student that his brother was either planning or currently involved in an act that was detrimental to the business and the spiritual well-being of the dreamer. A separation from the brother would be necessary as an act of self-protection. The result of this separation would be positive. This would all take place within the next two months.

I suggested that the student begin to extricate himself from business with his brother and further advised him that in order to remove the negativity that his brother was bringing into his life, he needed to invest in charitable work in the community.

Over the next few weeks, it was revealed that the student's brother was in fact making illegal purchases through the company. When he learned about it, the student confronted his brother—and with the aid and influence of their extended family, it was decided that the brother would leave the business and begin a new endeavor.

My Dream

Hopefully, as you have turned each page of this book, you have gradually discovered that dreams can be very potent instruments in guiding and directing us through the maze of life. Ever since I began delving deeply into the wisdom of Kabbalah, it has been my personal dream to share this wisdom and its tools with as many people as possible.

Think about this: We have a variety of tools that help us get along in life—computers, medicine, gyms, health food, and many more. And developments in technology have helped enrich our lives in various ways. From the first telegraph machine to the cell phone and the Internet, technology has helped us conquer time and space by allowing us to instantly communicate with people all over the world. But what tools or technology can we use to grow and to satisfy other aspects of our lives, to help us communicate with our own soul and the 99 percent reality? This question is the real reason I have been so excited and passionate about Kabbalah. Kabbalah is a technology—a technology for the soul. Kabbalah's various tools, such as The 72 Names of God, the Red String, the Zohar, and this Dream Book, offer us a methodology for enriching our lives and achieving our ultimate destiny, which is lasting fulfillment and joy. Although this technology is some 4000 years old, it is far more advanced than the latest discoveries of medical science and physics. But as the Kabbalists of history have constantly told us, the proof must be in the pudding. In other words, when we apply this technology to our lives, the results must be there 100 percent. If not, who needs Kabbalah? So I invite you to apply the insights of this book to your personal life and to dream big. Expect and demand results every step of the way. And remember, life is but a dream!

Other Symbols and Their Meaning—A Brief List

Dream	Interpretation
Common Themes	
Person who passed away gives us something	Positive; a channel to the Light
Snake	Positive; usually refers to money or sustenance
Tidal wave	Possible destruction
Sex with mother	Positive; elevating under-standing or spirituality
Egg	Positive; request heard
Flying	Positive; rising above your nature
Teeth falling out	Generally negative, in need of correction
Old boyfriend	Holding on to the past; an old issue becomes relevant again
Candle goes out	Need attention
Married but dreaming that you are unmarried	Real lack; not including partner in life; not sharing

Dream	Interpretation
Constructing a doorway	Marriage is forthcoming
Entering a metropolis	Your needs will be met
Unwalled city	Saved from trouble
Arrested	Guarded from harm
Looking out from a high place	Positive; long life
Needing to "pee"	Inability to express oneself in an area
Flying and then falling	Missing an opportunity
Car brakes don't work	Loss of control over life
Haircut; beard trim	Darkness to growth; a reference to the warmth of friends and family
Healthy person giving birth	Positive; extra life
The color baby blue	Negative; the result of ill will of another

House Dreams

Destroying your old house	Positive; moving forward spiritually
Building a new house	Positive
Moving to a beautiful house	Positive; spiritual vessel growing
Burning roof/wall falls	Possibly need correction

Dream	Interpretation
Tall buildings	Positive; the taller the better
Someone else's house	A message from that person for you
Former house	Holding on to the past; an old issue becomes relevant again
Living room	Problem with family
Bedroom	Problem with partner
Basement	Problem with sex life
Destroying a new house	Negative sign
Destroying an old house	Positive sign; moving forward
Well-decorated house	Positive; happiness and tranquillity
Wall falling in house	Negative; trouble is near
Going up to the roof	Positive; rising to eminence

Each room of a house can also refer to a particular part of the body.

Morbid Dreams

Person who passed away takes from us	Removing our ability to receive
Person who passed away takes our shoes	Negative; a correction is needed

Dream	Interpretation
Person who passed away kisses/cuddles	Positive
Person passed away bites	Needs attention
Person who passed away gives you a knife/gun	Positive; spiritually protected
Person who passed away passes away again	Need correction for a family member with that name
Fiancé passes away	Delay in marriage
Immediate family passes away	That person will have a longer life
Nonimmediate family passes away	Possibly need correction
Being buried	Losing money but NOT dying
You pass away	Positive; longer life

Animal Dreams

Bull or cow grazing	Better times coming
Bull or cow sleeping	Harder times coming
Camel	Saved from death
Pig	Increase in wealth
Horses	Strength or wisdom
Mule	Poverty

Dream	Interpretation
Wolf	Enemy rising
Mouse	Meeting someone new and significant
Scorpion	Dispute
Elephant	Positive; a request has been heard
Evil beasts	Lies told about you
Lion	Generally positive
Bees	Enemy attack
Flies	Robbery
Bird Dreams	
Goose	Honor; wisdom
Birds fighting	Quarrel
Eating a bird	Positive
Rooster	Male child imminent
Eagle	Greatness
Ravens	Movement toward understanding or sustenance
Owl	Loss
Seeing a hawk	Generally negative
Capturing a hawk	Very positive

Dream	Interpretation
Clothes Dreams	
Misplaced your clothes	Signifies a loss
Woman in man's clothes	She will inherit your riches
Black, red, or blue clothes	Can be trouble
Wearing a prayer shawl	You will marry
Wearing a royal crown	Good fortune will soon come to you
Torn clothes	A decree or judgment has been remove
Burned clothes	You will profit
Sewing clothes	Legal decision; often to do with building a house
Undressing when ill	Positive sign for spiritual or physical health
Dressed in silk	People will be jealous of you
Body Dreams	
Cannibalism	Beware of your hatred toward friends
Seeing yourself as dumb	Positive spiritual sign
Cut nipples	A sign of trouble
Blood from your body	Judgment being taken away
Beard ripped out	Gaining an evil reputation

Dream	Interpretation
Forearms	You will be loved
Seeing yourself ill	You will rejoice in the year
Seeing yourself becoming ritually pure	A negative sign
Barefoot	A loss
Nosebleed	Loss and recovery

For a free dream consultation or for more information or other technologies for the soul, please visit www.72.com—the official site of national best selling author Yehuda Berg—and discover the oldest technology in the world for affecting genuine transformation.

If you were inspired by this book in any way and would like to know how you can continue to enrich your life through the power of Kabbalah, here is what you can do next: Read the book *The Power of Kabbalah* or listen to the *Power of Kabbalah* audio tapes.

The Power of Kabbalah

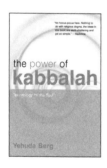

Imagine your life filled with unending joy, purpose, and contentment. Imagine your days infused with pure insight and energy. This is *The Power of Kabbalah*. It is the path from the momentary pleasure that most of us settle for, to the lasting fulfillment that is yours to claim. Your deepest desires are waiting to be realized. But they are not limited to the temporary rush from closing a business deal, the short-term high from drugs, or a passionate sexual relationship that lasts only a few short months.

Wouldn't you like to experience a lasting sense of wholeness and peace that is unshakable, no matter what may be happening around you? Complete fulfillment is the promise of Kabbalah. Within these pages, you will learn how to look at and navigate through life in a whole new way. You will understand your purpose and how to receive the abundant gifts waiting for you. By making a critical transformation from a reactive to a proactive being, you will increase your creative energy, get control of your life, and enjoy new spiritual levels of existence. Kabbalah's ancient teaching is rooted in the perfect union of the physical and spiritual laws already at work in your life. Get ready to experience this exciting realm of awareness, meaning, and joy.

The wonder and wisdom of Kabbalah has influenced the world's leading spiritual, philosophical, religious, and scientific minds. Until today, however, it was hidden away in ancient texts, available only to scholars who knew where to look. Now after many centuries, *The Power of Kabbalah* resides right here in this one remarkable book. Here, at long last is the complete and simple path—actions you can take right now to create the life you desire and deserve.

The Power of Kabbalah Audio Tapes

The Power of Kabbalah is nothing less than a user's guide to the universe. Move beyond where you are right now to where you truly want to be—emotionally, spiritually, creatively. This exciting tape series brings you the ancient, authentic teaching of Kabbalah in a powerful, practical audio format.

You can order these products from our Web site or by calling Student Support.

Student Support: Trained instructors are available 18 hours a day. These dedicated people are willing to answer any and all questions about Kabbalah and help guide you along in your effort to learn more. Just call **1-800-kabbalah**.

MORE PRODUCTS THAT CAN HELP YOU BRING THE WISDOM OF KABBALAH INTO YOUR LIFE

The 72 Names of God: Technology for the Soul™
By Yehuda Berg

The story of Moses and the Red Sea is well known to almost everyone; it's even been an Academy Award–winning film. What is not known, according to the internationally prominent author Yehuda Berg, is that a state-of-the-art technology is encoded and concealed within that biblical story. This technology is called the 72 Names of God, and it is the key—your key—to ridding yourself of depression, stress, creative stagnation, anger, illness, and other physical and emotional problems. In fact, the 72 Names of God is the oldest, most powerful tool known to mankind—far more powerful than any 21st century high-tech know-how when it comes to eliminating the garbage in your life so that you can wake up and enjoy life each day. Indeed, the 72 Names of God is the ultimate pill for anything and everything that ails you because it strikes at the DNA level of your soul.

The power of the 72 Names of God operates strictly on a soul level, not a physical one. It's about spirituality, not religiosity. Rather than being limited by the differences that divide people, the wisdom of the Names transcends humanity's age-old quarrels and belief systems to deal with the one common bond that unifies all people and nations: the human soul.

Becoming Like God
By Michael Berg

At the age of 16, Kabbalistic scholar Michael Berg began the herculean task of translating the *Zohar*, Kabbalah's chief text, from its original Aramaic into its first complete English translation. The *Zohar*, which consists of 23 volumes, is considered a compendium of virtually all information pertaining to the universe, and its wisdom is only beginning to be verified today.

During the ten years he worked on the *Zohar*, Michael Berg discovered the long-lost secret for which mankind has searched for more than 5,000 years: how to achieve our ultimate destiny. *Becoming Like God* reveals the transformative method by which people can actually break free of what is called "ego nature" to achieve total joy and lasting life.

Berg puts forth the revolutionary idea that for the first time in history, an opportunity is being made available to humankind: an opportunity to Become Like God.

The Secret
By Michael Berg

Like a jewel that has been painstakingly cut and polished, *The Secret* reveals life's essence in its most concise and powerful form. Michael Berg begins by showing you how our everyday understanding of our purpose in the world is literally backwards. Whenever there is pain in our lives—indeed, whenever there is anything less than complete joy and fulfillment—this basic misunderstanding is the reason.

The Essential Zohar
By Rav Berg

The *Zohar* has traditionally been known as the world's most esoteric and profound spiritual document, but Kabbalist Rav Berg, this generation's greatest living Kabbalist, has dedicated his life to making this wisdom universally available. The vast wisdom and Light of the *Zohar* came into being as a gift to all humanity, and *The Essential Zohar* at last explains this gift to the world.

Taming Chaos
By Rav Berg

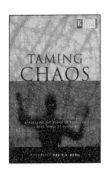

Eminent Kabbalist Rav Berg offers a deep, advanced explanation of how the tools of Kabbalah (Ana B'Koach, Kabbalistic Meditation, 72 Names and much more) can be used in everyday life to eliminate chaos.

Chaos is not only pandemonium in the streets and people running around like mad. It is personal chaos. The difficulties that you face each day, from stubbing your toe and getting stuck on long lines to losing money in business, having troubles in relationships and getting sick. Whatever it is that gets in the way of your happiness, this book will show you how to make it work for—not against—you.

Power of You
By Rav Berg

For the past 5,000 years, neither science nor psychology has been able to solve the fundamental problem of chaos in people's lives.

Now, one man is providing the answer. He is Kabbalist Rav Berg.

Beneath the pain and chaos that disrupts our lives, Kabbalist Rav Berg brings to light a hidden realm of order, purpose, and unity. Revealed is a universe in which mind becomes master over matter—a world in which God, human thought, and the entire cosmos are mysteriously interconnected.

Join this generation's premier Kabbalist on a mind-bending journey along the cutting edge of reality. Peer into the vast reservoir of spiritual wisdom that is Kabbalah, where the secrets of creation, life, and death have remained hidden for thousands of years.

THE KABBALAH CENTRE
The International Leader in the Education of Kabbalah

Since its founding, the Kabbalah Centre has had a single mission: to improve and transform people's lives by bringing the power and wisdom of Kabbalah to all who wish to partake of it.

Through the lifelong efforts of kabbalists Rav and Karen Berg, and the great spiritual lineage of which they are a part, an astonishing 3.5 million people around the world have already been touched by the powerful teachings of Kabbalah. And each year, the numbers are growing!

May our dreams always guide us towards
the Light, elevating our souls and making our
world a better place.

Sharon, Brandon and Mauricio Oberfeld